G000022616

101 ANSWERS TO
MONEY PROBLEMS

10 REASONS FOR INVESTING
35 WAYS OF SAVING SMARTLY
50 SMART IDEAS ON PROPERTY INVESTMENT

©2000 Matthew Ashimolowo

Published by Mattyson Media an imprint of MAMM

Matthew Ashimolowo Media Ministries
57 Waterden Road
Hackney Wick
London
E15 2EE

Bible quotes are from the King James Bible
unless otherwise stated.

ISBN 1 874 646 333

10 REASONS FOR INVESTING

Good years must pay for bad years.
Delayed gratification is important to achieve this.

Never have a zero month.
Profitable servants must always have left overs.

God gives seed so it can become trees.

Creating wealth for a purpose:
1. You must always prepare for the famine of old age.
2. The famine of being unmarketable.
3. To avoid prostituting yourself.

So that you can be a lender and not a borrower.

God who saved you from sin has given you the power to get wealth.

Clock all your money and what you are achieving.

One hundred pounds in the account of your new born baby at three point ninety five percent over twenty five years equals ten thousand pounds.

Kingdom promotion.

Leaving an inheritance.

To start and perpetuate generational blessing.

Providing for a future of comfort.

35 WAYS OF SAVING SMARTLY

Don't save until you clear credit card debt.

See clearing debt as a form of savings.

Shop around for the best in interest rate access and flexibility.

The rule of recovery is: clear debt , budget and save.

Have a standing order for money to go instantly to your deposit account from your current account.

Get ready to see welfare from the state cut to the barest minimum in the future.

A woman in her twenties who saves one hundred pounds monthly in a stock tracking account until her thirties and stops. When she is sixty she will have one point three million pounds.

If you save three pounds a day, and five hundred pounds a year, it will be one million pounds in forty years.

If you do not spend your daily one pound fifty pence on coffee, it will become three hundred and ninety pounds a year.

Savings is money accumulated by economising; while investment is putting out money for a higher return.

A personal pension scheme is a smart idea for anyone who is in the middle of a job change or is self-employed.

Everything you do early often comes cheaper.

Assess the damage you have done to your finances.
Go through your statements, including everything you owe.

Cut down the non-essentials immediately.

BUDGET -
for your future .
For example don't go Christmas shopping without a budget.

Make allowance for major expenses that are coming when budgeting.

Do not overdraw from your bank without authorisation.

Authorised overdraft attracts around twenty percent interest.

Unauthorised overdraft attracts around thirty percent interest.

Study the kind of bank account(s) you have.

Do they charge on a current account?
Do they pay interest on a current account?

Switch your mortgage to a cheaper lender.

Shop around for mortgage deals, but watch out for the penalties.

SPREAD.
Spread the big expenses over several months or weeks.

Do not economise what you put into your pension - so that you can rest in the evening of life.

Always cry out for help when you are in debt.

Unpaid bills, may end up in a bad credit reference, and creditors not being favourable.

Switch your credit card debt to a cheaper plastic.
Stop credit card loyalty.

Put your child's benefit in an ISA (Instant Savings Account) that is connected to the stock market.

Stablise your expenses to be in line with your level of income.

Spend less than you earn.

Don't move your spending to keep up with your income.
If you cannot handle a little, much will not come.

Through prayer and obedience to God, shut the door on the enemy who attacks your finances.

Maximise what you make.

Subsidise your income.

God will start you out with something small
- so get it right.
Your ability to manage one hundred pounds
affects the one thousand level.

Be practical to be profitable.

Look for your predominant gift area and stay there.

Three pounds a day or five hundred pounds a year at thirteen percent increase equals one million pounds after forty years.

Protect yourself, assets, and future through:

General Insurance.
Life Insurance.
Pension Scheme.
Health Insurance.

Shop around for a bank that works for you.

Live below your income.
If more than thirty percent of your income goes on rent, you are spending too much.

Start saving early - meaning now.

Dress your money up in work clothes.

Many families have monies lying idle in places. The U.S. treasury reports that one hundred and thirty four billion dollars is unaccounted for.

Find advisers who will not gain from their counsel.

6 INVESTMENT HANG-UPS

People do not invest because they tend to look for horror stories that confirm the negative hypothesis, they hold on investment.

People do not invest because they are busy comparing themselves to those who are not doing as well as they are.

People do not invest because they believe that a negative prediction on finance will be fulfilled soon.

Some take risks when the value of their stocks are going down, they delay instead of cutting their losses, they hold on and hope for a come back.

Some people's reaction to investment opportunity is too slow, too little, or too late.

The fear of losing, and the fear of regret often make people not to take action and invest.

50 SMART IDEAS ON PROPERTY INVESTMENT

Don't pay the standard variable rate for a mortgage - NEGOTIATE.

Don't change mortgage lenders if you can save thousands when buying a bigger property from the one on which you had a previous mortgage.

Despite the penalties attached to a fixed mortgage, search out if a switch to another lender will still pay in spite of penalties.

It is no crime to ring your lenders and ask if there is a deal that will save you money.

Check other lenders rates and perks before calling.

Go for capped rates without redemption penalties.

Search for lenders who may want to cover valuation and legal fees or alternatively who may give a large discount.

Use every spare cash to reduce your mortgage.

Every one hundred pounds paid in excess of a fixed mortgage equals three hundred and thirteen pounds, or minus two weeks off the total you are supposed to pay.

Every extra one thousand pounds equals five thousand pounds.

Consider letting out the old house or flat as you move to the new.

Do not let out without informing your mortgagors; they could penalise if you don't.

Beware of letting agents if you can - fifteen percent charge for letting is no small money.

Your insurers may need to know that you are letting out.

House prices can fall; stop borrowing all the time on the equity of your house.

Make sure there is good demand before you get involved in a buy-to-let mode.

Make higher repayments when you borrow against your home.

Think twice before borrowing against your house to finance a business.

Always use professionals who are qualified in their chosen field.

Lawyers, quantity surveyors, accountants and builders.

Always compare mortgage rates offered.

Do not be carried away by interior decoration; check for signs of ageing or building problems.

ie. cracks, settlement, dampness or woodworm.

Aim to pay earlier than the number of years on the mortgage.

Make effort to pay before the monthly due date on the mortgage.

When looking for property - consider the location.

Endeavour to cut down your monthly outlay in payments by having more than the five percent deposit required.

A leasehold is only okay if it is an investment property.

Check the terms of the contract if it is a leasehold.

Check for infestations of ants, rodents and cockroaches.

Ensure that there are no special covenants or charges on the land.

Do not set out to build overseas unless you can supervise the work, and if it is going to appreciate.

Do not invest in real estate overseas unless you are going to use it, and it should be where properties appreciate.

Look for properties which require little work, renovate and sell.

If you live overseas, be wise with your method of sending money for property purchase.

Always view real estate as an upward investment.

Real estate could be a means of generating income without much effort.

Avoid enticing mortgage schemes which have long term drawbacks.

Do not succumb to estate agent's language of pressure.

Remember if you can't sleep on a decision, it may not be worth it.

Know other extra costs in the area.
eg. council tax, insurance, etc.

View your potential property during day time.

Make sure your spouse puts your name on the document of the house.

The crime rate in an area can affect your home and content insurance?

Ask for a mortgage with daily interest rate calculation.

If in doubt about the quality of a building, pay for a structural survey.

You will spend little to avoid a nightmare.

Survey the building for subsidence or flooding if necessary.

Avoid co-ownership with housing trusts and associations if you can.

What level of local authority services are available to you?

Avoid listed buildings unless you are ready for the restrictions.

If you are selling, remember that every little work carried out will enhance the quality of your property.

When buying investment properties - try for a no deposit mortgage.

First time buyers should find a mortgage before finding the property.

Sign up with agents who have the kind of property you want.

Don't wait for agents to send you details - PURSUE.

SCRIPTURES ON FINANCE AND PROSPERITY

"Through wisdom is an house builded; and by understanding it is established: And by knowledge shall the chambers be filled with all precious and pleasant riches. A wise man is strong; yea, a man of knowledge increaseth strength. For by wise counsel thou shalt make thy war: and in multitude of counsellors there is safety.
Proverbs 24:3-6

"Give, and it shall be given unto you; good measure, pressed down, and shaken together, and running over, shall men give into your bosom. For with the same measure that ye mete withal it shall be measured to you again." Luke 6:38

"The thief cometh not, but for to steal, and to kill, and to destroy: I am come that they might have life, and that they might have it more abundantly."
John 10:10

"The righteous shall flourish like the palm tree: he shall grow like a cedar in Lebanon. Those that be planted in the house of the LORD shall flourish in the courts of our God. They shall still bring forth fruit in old age; they shall be fat and flourishing;"
Psalm 92:12-14

"The LORD will not suffer the soul of the righteous to famish: but he casteth away the substance of the wicked. He becometh poor that dealeth with a slack hand: but the hand of the diligent maketh rich."
Proverbs 10:3-4

*"My son, let not them depart from thine eyes: keep sound wisdom
and discretion: So shall they be life unto thy soul, and grace to thy neck. Then shalt
thou walk in thy way safely, and thy foot shall not stumble. When thou liest down, thou
shalt not be afraid: yea, thou shalt lie down, and thy sleep shall be sweet."*
Proverbs 3:21-24

*"In the house of the righteous is much treasure: but in the
revenues of the wicked is trouble."* *Proverbs 15:6*

*"The soul of the sluggard desireth, and hath nothing: but the soul of the diligent shall
be made fat."* *Proverbs 13:4*

*"Seest thou a man diligent in his business? he shall stand before
kings; he shall not stand before mean men."*
Proverbs 22:29

"Only be thou strong and very courageous, that thou mayest observe to do according to all the law, which Moses my servant commanded thee: turn not from it to the right hand or to the left, that thou mayest prosper withersoever thou goest. This book of the law shall not depart out of thy mouth; but thou shalt meditate therein day and night, that thou mayest observe to do according to all that is written therein: for then thou shalt make thy way prosperous, and then thou shalt have good success."
Joshua 1:7-8

"And keep the charge of the LORD thy God, to walk in his ways, to keep his statutes, and his commandments, and his judgments, and his testimonies, as it is written in the law of Moses, that thou mayest prosper in all that thou doest, and whithersoever thou turnest thyself:"
1 Kings 2:3

"Behold, God is mighty, and despiseth not any: he is mighty in strength and wisdom. He preserveth not the life of the wicked: but giveth right to the poor. He withdraweth not his eyes from the righteous: but with kings are they on the throne; yea, he doth establish them for ever, and they are exalted. And if they be bound in fetters, and be holden in cords of affliction; Then he sheweth them their work, and their transgressions that they have exceeded. He openeth also their ear to discipline, and commandeth that they return from iniquity. If they obey and serve him, they shall spend their days in prosperity, and their years in pleasures."

Job 36:5-11

"These have power to shut heaven, that it rain not in the days of their prophecy: and have power over waters to turn them to blood, and to smite the earth with all plagues, as often as they will."

Hebrews 11:6

"Let them shout for joy, and be glad, that favor my righteous cause: yea, let them say continually, Let the LORD be magnified, which hath pleasure in the prosperity of his servant." Psalm 35:27

"The LORD is my shepherd; I shall not want. He maketh me to lie down in green pastures: he leadeth me beside the still waters. He restoreth my soul: he leadeth me in the paths of righteousness for his name's sake.
Yea, though I walk through the valley of the shadow of death, I will fear no evil: for thou art with me; thy rod and thy staff they comfort me. Thou preparest a table before me in the presence of mine enemies: thou anointest my head with oil; my cup runneth over. Surely goodness and mercy shall follow me all the days of my life: and I will dwell in the house of the LORD for ever."
Psalm 23:1-6

"A good man leaveth an inheritance to his children's children: and the wealth of the sinner is laid up for the just."
Proverbs 13:22

"The eyes of all wait upon thee; and thou givest them their meat in due season. Thou openest thine hand, and satisfiest the desire of every living thing."
Psalm 145:15 -16

"And they rose early in the morning, and went forth into the wilderness of Tekoa: and as they went forth, Jehoshaphat stood and said, Hear me, O Judah, and ye inhabitants of Jerusalem; Believe in the LORD your God, so shall ye be established; believe his prophets, so shall ye prosper."
2 Chronicles 20:20

"And he sought God in the days of Zechariah, who had understanding in the visions of God: and as long as he sought the LORD, God made him to prosper." 2 Chronicles 26:5

"Beloved, I wish above all things that thou mayest prosper and be in health, even as thy soul prospereth. For I rejoiced greatly, when the brethren came and testified of the truth that is in thee, even as thou walkest in the truth. I have no greater joy than to hear that my children walk in truth."
3 John 2-4

"The thoughts of the diligent tend only to plenteousness; but of every one that is hasty only to want." Proverbs 21:5

"Bring ye all the tithes into the storehouse, that there may be meat in mine house, and prove me now herewith, saith the LORD of hosts, if I will not open you the windows of heaven, and pour you out a blessing, that there shall not be room enough to receive it. And I will rebuke the devourer for your sakes, and he shall not destroy the fruits of your ground; neither shall your vine cast her fruit before the time in the field, saith the LORD of hosts. And all nations shall call you blessed: for ye shall be a delightsome land, saith the LORD of hosts."
Malachi 3:10-12

"But my God shall supply all your need according to his riches in glory by Christ Jesus." Philippians 4:19

"In that night did God appear unto Solomon, and said unto him,
"Ask what I shall give thee. And Solomon said unto God, Thou hast shewed great mercy
unto David my father, and hast made me to reign in his stead. Now, O LORD God, let thy
promise unto David my father be established: for thou hast made me king over a
people like the dust of the earth in multitude. Give me now wisdom and knowledge, that I
may go out and come in before this people: for who can judge this thy people, that is so
great?
And God said to Solomon, Because this was in thine heart, and thou hast not asked riches,
wealth, or honor, nor the life of thine enemies, neither yet hast asked long life; but hast
asked wisdom and knowledge for thyself, that thou mayest judge my people, over whom I
have made thee king: Wisdom and knowledge is granted unto thee; and I will give thee
riches, and wealth, and honor, such as none of the kings have had that have been before
thee, neither shall there any after thee have the like."
2 Chronicles 1:7-12

"Honor the LORD with thy substance, and with the firstfruits of all thine increase: So shall thy barns be filled with plenty, and thy presses shall burst out with new wine." Proverbs 3:9,10

"He that giveth unto the poor shall not lack: but he that hideth his eyes shall have many a curse." Proverbs 28:27

"He that hath a bountiful eye shall be blessed; for he giveth of his bread to the poor." Proverbs 22:9

"If ye walk in my statutes, and keep my commandments, and do them; Then I will give you rain in due season, and the land shall yield her increase, and the trees of the field shall yield their fruit. For I will have respect unto you, and make you fruitful, and multiply you, and establish my covenant with you. And ye shall eat old store, and bring forth the old because of the new."
Leviticus 26:3-4, 9-10

Now therefore perform the doing of it; that as there was a readiness to will, so there may be a performance also out of that which ye have. For if there be first a willing mind, it is accepted according to that a man hath, and not according to that he hath not."
2 Corinthians 8:11-12

"For as the rain cometh down, and the snow from heaven, and returneth not thither, but watereth the earth, and maketh it bring forth and bud, that it may give seed to the sower, and bread to the eater: So shall my word be that goeth forth out of my mouth: it shall not return unto me void, but it shall accomplish that which I please, and it shall prosper in the thing whereto I sent it. For ye shall go out with joy, and be led forth with peace: the mountains and the hills shall break forth before you into singing, and all the trees of the field shall clap their hands. Instead of the thorn shall come up the fir tree, and instead of the brier shall come up the myrtle tree: and it shall be to the LORD for a name, for an everlasting sign that shall not be cut off."
Isaiah 55:10-13

"Moreover, brethren, we do you to wit of the grace of God bestowed on the churches of Macedonia; How that in a great trial of affliction the abundance of their joy and their deep poverty abounded unto the riches of their liberality. For to their power, I bear record, yea, and beyond their power they were willing of themselves; Praying us with much intreaty that we would receive the gift, and take upon us the fellowship of the ministering to the saints. And this they did, not as we hoped, but first gave their own selves to the Lord, and unto us by the will of God. Insomuch that we desired Titus, that as he had begun, so he would also finish in you the same grace also. Therefore, as ye abound in every thing, in faith, and utterance, and knowledge, and in all diligence, and in your love to us, see that ye abound in this grace also. I speak not by commandment, but by occasion of the forwardness of others, and to prove the sincerity of your love. For ye know the grace of our Lord Jesus Christ, that, though he was rich, yet for your sakes he became poor, that ye through his poverty might be rich. And herein I give my advice: for this is expedient for you, who have begun before, not only to do, but also to be forward a year ago. 2 Corinthians 8:1-10

"He that covereth his sins shall not prosper: but whoso confesseth and forsaketh them shall have mercy." Proverbs 28:13

"There is that scattereth, and yet increaseth; and there is that withholdeth more than is meet, but it tendeth to poverty. The liberal soul shall be made fat: and he that watereth shall be watered also himself. He that withholdeth corn, the people shall curse him: but blessing shall be upon the head of him that selleth it."
Proverbs 11:24-26

"The rich ruleth over the poor, and the borrower is servant to the lender." Proverbs 22:7

"And Abram was very rich in cattle, in silver, and in gold.!"
Genesis 13:2

"The thoughts of the diligent tend only to plenteousness; but of every one that is hasty only to want." Proverbs 21:5

"By humility and the fear of the LORD are riches, and honor, and life." Proverbs 22:4

"Cast thy bread upon the waters: for thou shalt find it after many days." Ecclesiastes 11:1

"He that oppresseth the poor to increase his riches, and he that giveth to the rich, shall surely come to want." Proverbs 22:16

"Poverty and shame shall be to him that refuseth instruction: but he that regardeth reproof shall be honored." Proverbs 13:18

"He that tilleth his land shall have plenty of bread: but he that followeth after vain persons shall have poverty enough. A faithful man shall abound with blessings: but he that maketh haste to be rich shall not be innocent."
Proverbs 28:19-20

"If any of you lack wisdom, let him ask of God, that giveth to all men liberally, and upbraideth not; and it shall be given him. But let him ask in faith, nothing wavering. For he that wavereth is like a wave of the sea driven with the wind and tossed."
James 1:5-6

"Then shalt thou delight thyself in the LORD; and I will cause thee to ride upon the high places of the earth, and feed thee with the heritage of Jacob thy father: for the mouth of the LORD hath spoken it." *Isaiah 58:14*

"But of him are ye in Christ Jesus, who of God is made unto us wisdom, and righteousness, and sanctification, and redemption:"
1 Corinthians 1:30

"But thou shalt remember the LORD thy God: for it is he that giveth thee power to get wealth, that he may establish his covenant which he sware unto thy fathers, as it is this day. And it shall be, if thou do at all forget the LORD thy God, and walk after other gods, and serve them, and worship them, I testify against you this day that ye shall surely perish."
Deuteronomy 8:18,19

"For bodily exercise profiteth little: but godliness is profitable unto all things, having promise of the life that now is, and of that which is to come."
1 Timothy 4:8

"The rich man's wealth is his strong city: the destruction of the poor is their poverty. The blessing of the LORD, it maketh rich, and he addeth no sorrow with it. The fear of the wicked, it shall come upon him: but the desire of the righteous shall be granted."
Proverbs 10:15,22,24

"If ye be willing and obedient, ye shall eat the good of the land:" *Isaiah 1:19*

"Do not err, my beloved brethren. very good gift and every perfect gift is from above, and cometh down from the Father of lights, with whom is no variableness, neither shadow of turning."
James 1:16, 17

"Keep therefore the words of this covenant, and do them, that ye may prosper in all that ye do." *Deuteronomy 29:9*

"And it shall come to pass, if thou shalt hearken diligently unto the voice of the LORD thy God, to observe and to do all his commandments which I command thee this day, that the LORD thy God will set thee on high above all nations of the earth: And all these blessings shall come on thee, and overtake thee, if thou shalt hearken unto the voice of the LORD thy God. Blessed shalt thou be in the city, and blessed shalt thou be in the field. Blessed shall be the fruit of thy body, and the fruit of thy ground, and the fruit of thy cattle, the increase of thy kine, and the flocks of thy sheep. Blessed shall be thy basket and thy store. Blessed shalt thou be when thou comest in, and blessed shalt thou be when thou goest out. The LORD shall cause thine enemies that rise up against thee to be smitten before thy face: they shall come out against thee one way, and flee before thee seven ways. The LORD shall command the blessing upon thee in thy storehouses, and in all that thou settest thine hand unto; and he shall bless thee in the land which the LORD thy God giveth thee.

Deuteronomy 28:1-8